Exploring Space

Written by
Cynthia Pratt Nicolson

Illustrated by
Bill Slavin

Kids Can Press

To Donald

Acknowledgments

I am grateful to the many scientists who have donated their time and expertise to the Starting with Space series. Their enthusiasm has been infectious and has strengthened my own wonder at the enormity of space and our human efforts to probe its depths. My thanks go to Dr. Ellis Miner at NASA for his helpful advice on this book. Any errors that may have crept in are my responsibility. I would also like to thank Jurrie van der Woude at the NASA Jet Propulsion Laboratory and James Hartsfield at the Johnson Space Center for their kind assistance.

I am grateful to Valerie Hussey at Kids Can Press for giving me the opportunity to write about this exciting topic, and to Lori Burwash, Laura Ellis and Val Wyatt for their cheerful, capable editing. Bill Slavin's excellent illustrations have added warmth and humor to each book in the series. Thanks, Bill! Finally, I would like to thank my family and friends for their continued interest and support.

Kids Can Press acknowledges the support of the Ontario Arts Council, the Canada Council for the Arts and the Government of Canada, through BPIDP, for our publishing activity.

Published in Canada by
Kids Can Press Ltd.
29 Birch Avenue
Toronto, ON M4V 1E2

Published in the U.S. by
Kids Can Press Ltd.
4500 Witmer Estates
Niagara Falls, NY 14305-1386

Edited by Laura Ellis, Val Wyatt and Lori Burwash
Designed by Marie Bartholomew and Esperança Melo
Printed in Hong Kong by Wing King Tong Co. Ltd.

Photo Credits
NASA/Space Telescope Science Institute (STScI)/Association of Universities for Research in Astronomy: page 4
NASA: pages 14, 18 (both), 20, 22 (both), 29
Canadian Space Agency: page 16 (artist's conception)
NASA/Jet Propulsion Laboratory: pages 24, 26 (artist's conception), 30 (both), 31 (both)
NASA/U.S. Geological Survey: page 25
NASA/STScI: pages 32, 33 (all)
National Radio Astronomy Observatory: page 34

CM 00 0 9 8 7 6 5 4 3 2 1
CM PA 00 0 9 8 7 6 5 4 3 2 1

Canadian Cataloguing in Publication Data

Nicolson, Cynthia Pratt
    Exploring space

(Starting with space)
Includes index.
ISBN 1-55074-711-8 (bound)   ISBN 1-55074-713-4 (pb)

1. Astronautics—Juvenile literature. 2. Outer space—Explorati —Juvenile literature. I. Slavin, Bill. II. Title. III. Series.

TL793.N52 2000   j629.4   C99-933010

Kids Can Press is a Nelvana company

Contents

Searching from Earth

Space is amazing. It stretches farther than you can imagine and contains more stars than you could ever count. For centuries, people have gazed at the sky and wondered, "What's out there?" Long ago, they told stories to explain what they saw.

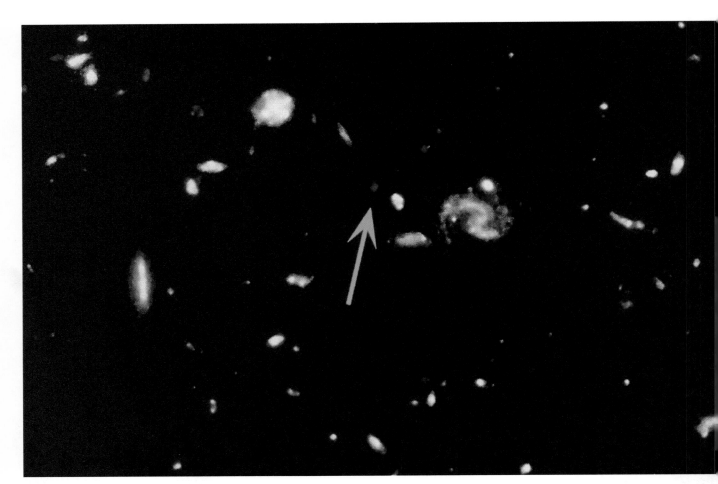

The Hubble Space Telescope took this photo of deep space. Each spot of light contains millions of stars. The arrow points to a faint glow believed to be the farthest galaxy ever seen.

Early space story

The Cahto people of northern California told this story of how the Sun, Moon and stars came to be in the sky.

One day, Coyote woke up to find the world in complete darkness. The Sun was trapped inside the house of an old woman.

"I must bring light back to the people," said Coyote.

"We will help you," squeaked three mice who were nearby.

Coyote threw a blanket over his head and approached the woman's house. The mice scampered after him.

"I'm a poor, tired traveler," Coyote said to the woman. "Please give me a place to sleep."

Tricked by Coyote's charming voice, the old woman let him in. Coyote began to sing a lullaby and, within moments, the woman was fast asleep. Looking around, Coyote soon found the Sun lying in a corner. It was covered with a blanket and tied down with leather straps.

"We can handle this," said the mice. They gnawed and gnawed until the straps were split apart.

Then Coyote grabbed the Sun. He ran outside and cut the glowing ball into pieces.

Using one leather strap for a slingshot, Coyote flung many tiny pieces of the Sun into the sky. These were the stars. He used a larger chunk to make the Moon. What was left became the Sun we know today. People were overjoyed with the bright and beautiful sky Coyote had created. They showered him with gifts and promised to tell his story forever.

If you see a word you don't know, look it up in the glossary on page 39.

How did people first learn about space?

Early sky watchers tracked the Sun, Moon, stars and the planets visible to the naked eye: Mercury, Venus, Mars, Jupiter and Saturn. People learned to predict the seasons and phases of the Moon. Based on this knowledge, they created calendars.

Although people long ago knew a lot about the sky, they had ideas that were mistaken. Most believed that the Sun and the planets revolved around Earth. Ancient Greeks thought the Sun, Moon, planets and stars were embedded in hollow glass spheres nested one inside the other.

In 1543, a Polish astronomer named Copernicus wrote tha all the planets, includi Earth, circle the Sun At the time, very few people believed him.

Where is space?

Space begins about 120 km (75 mi.) above Earth's surface. This is where the atmosphere, a blanket of gases surrounding Earth, becomes very thin. If you could drive a car straight up into the sky at highway speed, you would reach space in less than two hours.

TRY IT!
Create a constellation

When ancient people looked up at the stars, they imagined pictures in the sky. They described animals, gods and people outlined by stars. Each group of stars was called a constellation. You can make up your own constellations and stories.

You'll need:
- a small foam meat tray
- a craft knife (Ask an adult to help you use this.)
- a clear night
- a place away from bright lights
- an old blanket or reclining lawn chair

1. Make a star-viewing frame by cutting a square in the center of the meat tray. The hole should be about 10 cm (4 in.) on each side.

2. Go outside and make yourself comfortable looking up at the sky.

3. Use your frame to view different groups of stars. When you find a group you like, imagine what its shape might represent. Does it remind you of a person? An animal? A cartoon character?

4. Give your constellation a name. Invent a story about how it came to be in the sky.

The 88 constellations recognized by modern astronomers were named by people who lived long, long ago.

Who invented the telescope?

In 1608, Dutch eyeglass maker Hans Lippershey constructed the first telescope. His basic design — two lenses in a tube — was improved by Galileo Galilei, a scientist in Venice.

With his new telescope, Galileo spotted four moons circling the planet Jupiter. This discovery convinced him that Earth was not the center of the universe. Powerful people of the time were shocked by Galileo's ideas. They confined him to his house for the last years of his life.

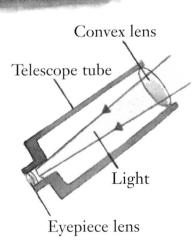

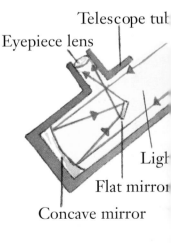

About 350 years ago, Sir Isaac Newton discovered how gravity pulls on objects in space. His method for calculating the path of a moving object is still used to aim spacecraft at the Moon and planets.

How do telescopes work?

Telescopes bend light to make things appear closer. In a *refracting* telescope, a convex (outward curving) lens focuses light, and the eyepiece lens magnifies the image. In a *reflecting* telescope, a concave (inward curving) mirror focuses light on a flat mirror that reflects the image to the eyepiece.

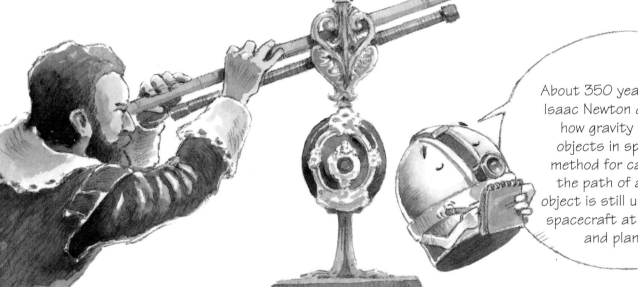

Convex lens

Telescope tube

Light

Eyepiece lens

A refracting telescope

Telescope tube

Eyepiece lens

Light

Flat mirror

Concave mirror

A reflecting telescope

Some of the earliest recorded sky observations were scratched into clay tablets by the Akkadians, who lived about 4500 years ago in what is now the Middle East.

With a strong pair of binoculars, you can see everything Galileo saw with his homemade telescope.

Early Polynesians used the stars to guide them on their voyages from island to island in the Pacific Ocean.

The first asteroid was discovered in 1801 by an Italian monk named Giuseppe Piazzi.

What did telescopes reveal about space?

Telescopes allowed astronomers to peer farther into space than ever before. In 1781, in England, astronomer William Herschel discovered the planet Uranus. In 1846, two astronomers at the Berlin Observatory pointed their telescope toward a spot where others had predicted a new planet would be — and found Neptune. The last planet in our solar system to be discovered was Pluto. It was found in 1930 by Clyde Tombaugh at the Lowell Observatory in Arizona.

Telescopes also gave people a new understanding of the stars. By 1923, astronomers had discovered that many spots of light in the sky aren't single stars at all. They are huge groups of stars called galaxies.

What have we learned about our galaxy?

We live in a galaxy called the Milky Way. It contains about 200 billion stars like our Sun. These stars form an enormous orbiting spiral in space.

Before the 20th century, people thought the Sun was the center of the Milky Way. By 1920, astronomers had figured out that our solar system is a tiny dot in one of the Milky Way's arms. The old idea that Earth was the center of the universe was laid to rest forever.

The Milky Way is also the name given to the cloudy band of light we see in the night sky when we look deep into our galaxy.

Our Solar System

Sun
Mercury
Venus
Earth
Mars
Jupiter
Saturn
Uranus
Neptune
Pluto

TRY IT!
Swirl a spiral galaxy

Our galaxy, the Milky Way, is constantly spinning. This rotating motion may have produced its pinwheel shape. In this activity, you can watch a swirling spiral take shape before your eyes.

> **You'll need:**
> - a cup of black coffee
> - a spoon
> - cream

1. Stir the coffee several times in one direction. It should keep spinning when you remove the spoon.

2. Slowly pour a small amount of cream into the coffee. Don't stir.

3. Watch the cream swirl into the coffee. Imagine you are a space traveler looking back at the Milky Way from a galaxy far, far away. Can you imagine seeing our Sun in one of its spiral arms?

We live in the Orion arm of the Milky Way. Our solar system takes about 240 million years to complete one full spin with the rest of the galaxy.

Orion arm   Sun

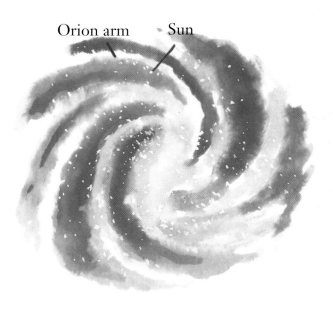

Blasting into space

Have you ever longed to know what's inside a gift-wrapped box? For centuries, people have had that same curiosity about space. Long before the days of rockets and spaceships, people dreamed of zooming into the sky to explore its mysteries.

An ancient astronaut

A daring space flight leads to danger in this Greek myth.

Icarus had been thrown into prison with his father, Daedalus. Escape seemed impossible, until Daedalus had an idea.

"We will fly away from here," he told his young son.

Icarus was astounded, but he helped his father gather feathers from birds that landed on the prison roof. He watched as Daedalus laid the feathers in rows and joined them with drops of melted wax. When the wax had hardened, Daedalus attached the rows of feathers to wooden frames. Soon he had created two sets of enormous wings.

"Strap them on like this," Daedalus said to Icarus. "And slowly flap your arms."

At first, Icarus was too excited, and his wings flapped wildly. Then he learned to control his arm motions. Soon he was flying behind his father.

But Icarus refused to fly steadily. He dipped down to the ocean and soared into the sky. Each time, he rose higher.

"I'm going to touch the Sun!" he called to his father.

"No, Icarus! Come back!" roared Daedalus. But it was too late.

As soon as Icarus went near the Sun, feathers began to drop from his wings. The Sun's heat melted the wax holding his wings together. Without wings, Icarus plunged into the ocean and was never seen again.

When were rockets invented?

Rockets were invented hundreds of years ago in China. They were fueled with gunpowder and used to launch fireworks and weapons. In 1903, Russian scientist Konstantin Tsiolkovsky proposed that rockets be used to explore space. But solid-fuel rockets did not have enough power to soar above Earth's atmosphere.

American scientist Robert Goddard experimented with rocket shapes and fuels, including more powerful liquid fuel. In 1926, he sent the first liquid-fuel rocket a short distance across his aunt's farm. Goddard continued to improve his early designs. His ideas are still used in space-rocket construction.

How do rockets work?

Burning fuel produces hot gases that rush out the back of a rocket and push it forward. Because rockets use so much fuel, they are built in sections, or stages. Each stage falls away after it is used up. This way, a much lighter spacecraft can reach orbit or outer space.

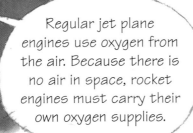

Regular jet plane engines use oxygen from the air. Because there is no air in space, rocket engines must carry their own oxygen supplies.

A *Saturn V* rocket launches *Apollo 11* on its journey to the Moon.

TRY IT!
Make a two-stage balloon rocket

You'll need:
- a paper or foam cup
- scissors
- a long balloon
- a round balloon

1. Remove the bottom of the cup with the scissors.

2. Partially blow up the long balloon. Don't tie it closed.

3. Put the open end of the long balloon into the cup and pull it out the bottom. Fold the end over the side of the cup and hold it tightly so air doesn't escape.

4. Push the round balloon up through the bottom of the cup. Leave its open end sticking out the bottom.

5. Blow up the round balloon and squeeze it closed without tying it.

6. To launch your rocket, release the round balloon.

The balloons work like rocket engines, propelling their load forward when gases escape out the back. (The balloons' gas is the air you blew into them.) The round balloon launches the cup like the first stage of a real rocket. When the round balloon is empty, the long balloon takes over, just like a rocket's second stage.

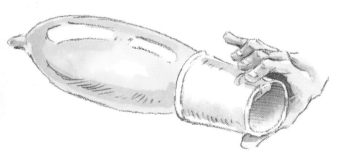

What was the first thing sent into space?

The first object launched into space was *Sputnik 1*, a silvery sphere the size of a large beach ball. *Sputnik* was launched from the former Soviet Union (now Russia) on October 4, 1957. It beeped out a radio signal that was picked up on Earth. This first artificial satellite orbited for 92 days and then fell back into Earth's atmosphere and burned up.

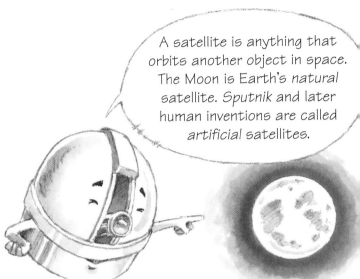

A satellite is anything that orbits another object in space. The Moon is Earth's *natural* satellite. *Sputnik* and later human inventions are called *artificial* satellites.

What do satellites do?

Since the 1960s, hundreds of artificial satellites have been launched into orbit. They gather signals from Earth and space and reflect these to collecting dishes on the ground. Using satellite signals, airplane pilots and ship captains can navigate more accurately. Astronomers can learn more about space, and other scientists can track the weather, forest fires or pollution. Satellites also transmit long-distance phone calls and radio programs. Some even deliver the signals for your favorite TV shows.

The Canadian satellite RADARSAT observes Earth from space. It tracks chang in the environment.

TRY IT!

See satellites in the night sky

1. Make yourself comfortable staring straight up at the sky. Watch for a tiny starlike dot that takes about a minute to cross the sky above your head. You are looking at a satellite orbiting Earth. (A distant plane will appear to move much more slowly.)

2. Watch for a satellite that gradually fades from view. It is moving from sunlight into Earth's shadow.

3. You may see a satellite that appears to blink on and off as it travels across the sky. You're probably looking at a spinning satellite that has one shiny side and one dark side.

You will see more satellites in summer than in winter. That's because satellites glow when the Sun glints off their shiny surfaces. In summer, your part of the world is tilted toward the Sun. During the first few hours of night, satellites can still catch and reflect the Sun's rays.

For more information about satellites and satellite viewing, visit this site on the Internet: http://liftoff.msfc.nasa.gov/academy/rocket_sci/satellites

Who was the first person in space?

On April 12, 1961, Major Yuri Gagarin of the former Soviet Union became the first human to fly into space. Gagarin's spacecraft, *Vostok 1*, circled Earth once.

In Russia, someone who travels into space is called a cosmonaut.

Who was the first person on the Moon?

On July 20, 1969, American Neil Armstrong became the first person to walk on the Moon.

Armstrong flew to the Moon in *Apollo 11* with Michael Collins and Buzz Aldrin. While Collins stayed in the main spacecraft, Armstrong and Aldrin descended to the Moon's surface. They planted an American flag and collected rocks and soil. Then they rejoined Collins and returned to Earth, landing safely on July 24.

In 1957, a Russian dog named Laika became the first living being launched into space. Laika did not survive her journey.

Astronaut Neil Armstrong took this photo of Buzz Aldrin and their landing craft on the Moon's surface.

An astronaut explores the Moon in the lunar rover, or "Moon buggy," during the *Apollo 17* mission.

TRY IT!
Measure your Moon strength

You'll need:
- 6 books*
- 6 cans of food*
- 6 shoes*
- a large cardboard box

* Use items that are about the same size as the other items in the same category.

1. Place all the items in the box.

2. Lift the box by crouching down and then straightening your legs. (This will protect your back.) Notice how heavy the box feels.

3. Take out five of each item. Leave only one book, one can and one shoe in the box.

4. Pretend you are on the Moon and the box still holds all the items. Lift the box again. How much lighter does it feel?

Because the Moon's mass is six times less than that of Earth, its pulling force — gravity — is only ⅙ as strong. That means things on the Moon weigh just ⅙ of their Earth weight. In other words, lifting a large object would be six times easier on the Moon.

Space Challenge: How much would you weigh on the Moon? (Answer on page 39.)

How do astronauts prepare for space?

Astronauts train hard. They exercise every day. As well, they learn all about their spacecraft and any experiments to be done during their mission.

To experience something like near-weightlessness, NASA astronauts put on space suits and enter an enormous water-filled tank. They also take short flights on a special jet that rises, then drops quickly, creating a few seconds of weightlessness. Astronauts call the jet the "Vomit Comet."

Underwater training helps astronauts prepare for space.

Why do astronauts feel weightless?

Astronauts float freely in a spacecraft orbiting Earth. So does everything else on board that isn't fastened down. This weightlessness — or "microgravity" — occurs because the spacecraft is continually falling toward Earth at the same time as it is zooming forward. Scientists say microgravity occurs because the spacecraft is in "free fall."

You may briefly feel weightlessness if you're in an elevator that drops rapidly. Do you understand why some astronauts feel sick on their first few days in space?

What do astronauts wear?

Inside a spacecraft, astronauts wear shirts and pants with many pockets. Outside, they need space suits that provide oxygen, pressure and protection from harmful sunlight. During launch and reentry, astronauts wear "partial pressure" suits, in case of emergency.

The "primary life support system" provides oxygen and pressure. It pumps cooling liquid through plastic tubes in the astronaut's inner suit.

The MMU (manned maneuvering unit) lets the astronaut fly outside the spacecraft. The astronaut can go forward, reverse, turn around and flip over.

helmet protects e astronaut from icrometeoroids oits of dust and ock in space) and olar rays. Inside, ere is a special p with a headset.

teel ball earings in the it's joints low the tronaut to ove freely.

The control device lets the astronaut check that the suit is working properly.

Molded gloves protect the astronaut's hands and can be equipped with special tools.

What is a space shuttle?

A space shuttle is a reusable spacecraft. It works like a combined spaceship and airplane that carries astronauts into orbit around Earth. (Space shuttles are not used for more distant journeys, such as those to the Moon.) When it lands, the shuttle glides down onto a runway.

Columbia was the first space shuttle to be launched, in April 1981.

With all rockets firing, the shuttle *Columbia* blasts off from the launchpad.

What is a space station?

A space station is a laboratory in space where astronauts live and work for months at a time. The first space station was launched by the former Soviet Union in 1971. In 1998, several countries began constructing the International Space Station. When finished, it will be a top-notch lab where seven astronauts can perform experiments and observe Earth from space.

American astronaut Shannon Lucid spent six months on the Russian space station *Mir* in 1996. Here she floats freely in the station's microgravity environment.

SPACE DATA

Alan Shepard was the first American in space. His 15-minute flight in 1961 ended with a splashdown in the Atlantic Ocean.

Valentina Tereshkova of the former Soviet Union was the first woman in space. She orbited Earth 45 times in 1963.

In 1962, John Glenn became the first American to orbit Earth. In 1998, at the age of 77, Glenn became the world's oldest astronaut when he flew on the space shuttle *Discovery*.

The worst-ever space disaster happened on January 28, 1986. Less than two minutes after liftoff, the *Challenger* space shuttle exploded, killing all seven astronauts on board.

Exploring the solar system

How do you explore a place that's too dangerous or distant for humans? Send in the robots! In the past 40 years, robotic spacecraft have transformed our ideas about far-off planets — and other parts of our vast solar system.

Mariner 10 took more than 3000 photos of Venus in 1974.

A Martian mystery

Is there life on other planets? Astronomers are still searching for the answer. Here's how one curious astronomer was tricked by his own lenses.

In 1877, Italian astronomer Giovanni Schiaparelli was observing Mars through a large telescope when he noticed a pattern of straight lines crisscrossing the planet's surface. Schiaparelli called these lines *canali*. This Italian word means "channels," but it was translated by English newspapers as "canals." The difference was important. While channels may happen naturally, canals are built.

Percival Lowell, a wealthy American astronomer, heard that Schiaparelli had seen canals on Mars. Determined to see for himself, Lowell built an observatory in Arizona. He peered through the powerful telescope and, sure enough, there were the canals.

Lowell guessed that Martians had built these canals to bring water from polar ice caps to their farms and cities. Over the next few years, he mapped more than 500 canals and wrote a book about life on Mars.

The canal idea was fascinating, but it was false. Other astronomers could not see what Lowell described. Recent space probes have returned close-up photos of Mars. They show valleys and canyons, but no canals.

What is a space probe?

A space probe is a robotic spacecraft with no people on board. It can travel much farther, and stay in space much longer, than a spacecraft with a human crew. A space probe is powered by nuclear or solar energy and is remotely controlled from Earth by radio signals.

Probes gather data by taking photographs and using radar to measure landforms. Some gather soil and air samples. Others perform experiments to detect signs of life. Without space probes we would know much less about our neighbors in space.

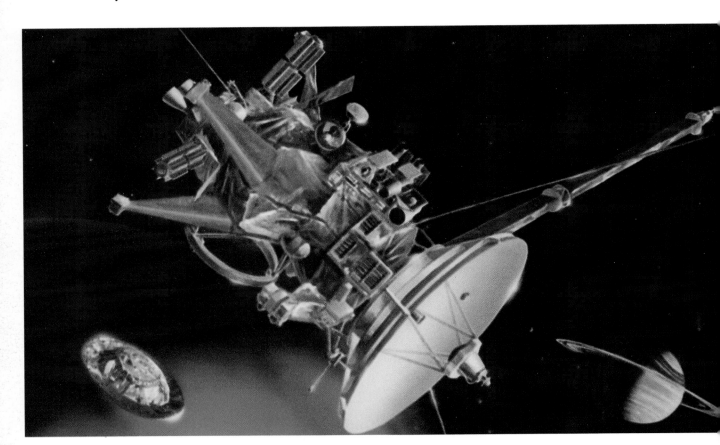

The space probe *Cassini* is scheduled to reach Saturn in 2004. It will study the planet's moons and rings.

How does a space probe send data to Earth?

A space probe uses radio signals to beam information to Earth. These signals are in the digital form computers use. Some signals produce images that show a distant planet's surface. Others carry information about the planet's temperature and atmosphere.

TRY IT!
Decode a binary message

Space probes communicate with computers using just two radio signals — on and off. To record this binary code, scientists use "1" for "on" and "0" for "off." Solve this binary puzzle to see an amazing discovery from an imaginary space probe.

> **You'll need:**
> ○ a sheet of graph paper
> ○ a pencil

1. On the paper, outline a rectangle that is 9 small squares across and 13 small squares down.

2. Starting in the upper left corner of your rectangle, follow this line of binary code. Shade in a square for every "1" and leave an empty square for every "0." When you reach a "/" go back to the left side for the next line. (You may find it easier to have someone read the signals out loud as you shade in the squares.)
010000010/001000100/000111000/001010100/000101000/100010001/011101110/000111000/000101000/011111110/100101001/000101000/0011 01100

3. If you have followed the code carefully, your space message will form a picture. What do you see? (Answer on page 39.)

What have space probes revealed about the Moon and the Sun?
Until 1959, no one had seen the far side of the Moon. That year, the Soviet probe *Luna 3* took photos of the Moon's hidden face. The photos showed lots of craters, but no large lava flood plains (which form the dark patches we see on the side facing Earth).

The American probe *Ulysses* passed over the Sun's south pole in 1994 and its north pole in 1995. *Ulysses* discovered that the Sun is surrounded by a huge magnetic field and that its solar winds can reach incredible speeds of up to 3.2 million km/h (2 million m.p.h.)

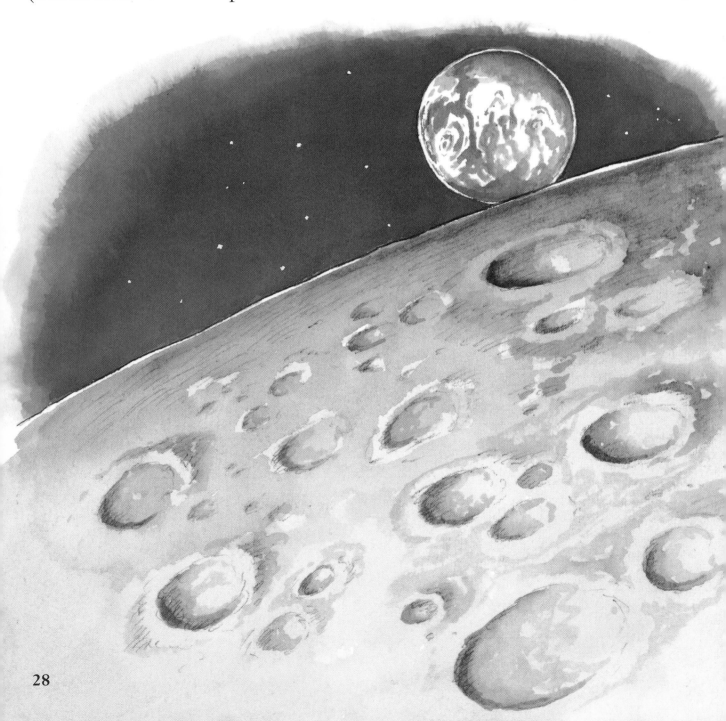

What have space probes discovered about comets and asteroids?

When Comet Halley reappeared in 1986, both Soviet and European probes were sent to take a closer look. The European probe *Giotto* photographed the comet's nucleus, a lumpy mixture of ice and rock about 16 km (10 mi.) long. Geysers of gas and dust blasted out of Halley's nucleus whenever the Sun's rays penetrated its core.

The *Galileo* space probe passed close by the asteroid Ida in 1991.

Photos showed that Ida has its own tiny moon.

The *Galileo* probe took this photo of asteroid Ida and its mini-moon, Dactyl.

SPACE DATA

If you wanted to visit Venus, you would have to travel 130 times farther than the Moon astronauts. A visit to Pluto would be 15 thousand times farther still.

The *Mars Observer* probe was launched in 1992. Just as it was about to go into orbit around Mars, the probe stopped signaling. NASA experts tried to make contact with the silent spacecraft, but *Mars Observer* was never heard from again.

Voyagers 1 and *2* are now beyond all the planets. They continue to send back data about the outskirts of our solar system.

What planetary secrets have space probes revealed?

More than 40 successful space probes have explored the planets of our solar system. Here are some astonishing things they've found.

Saturn, the second-largest planet, was visited by *Voyager*s *1* and *2* in 1980. The probes showed that Saturn's broad rings are made of hundreds of thinner rings. They also revealed 8 more moons, bringing Saturn's total to 18.

Jupiter, the largest planet, surprised scientists in 1979. Two *Voyager* probes revealed a thin ring circling this giant ball of gases. In 1994, when pieces of Comet Shoemaker-Levy 9 crashed into Jupiter, *Galileo* took photos and sent them back to Earth.

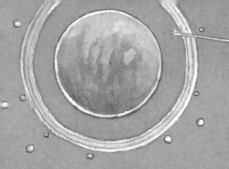

Uranus is so far from Earth
that little was known about
this blue-green gas planet
until *Voyager 2* flew by in
1986. The probe discovered
11 rings and 10 of Uranus's
17 moons.

Neptune, almost a
twin of Uranus in size,
was inspected by
Voyager 2 in 1989.
The probe measured
winds up to 1120 km/h
(700 m.p.h.) — the
fastest on any planet.

Pluto has not yet been
visited by a space probe,
but the *Pluto-Kuiper
Express* is being prepared
for a send-off in 2004. In
spite of its speedy name,
the probe will take about
ten years to reach the
distant planet.

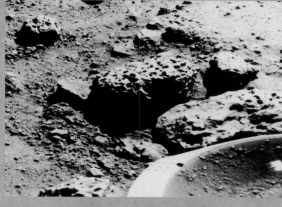

Mars has been explored by many
probes, including *Pathfinder* in 1997.
The missions showed that Mars may
once have had flowing water, but
none has found any form of life.

Venus has always been hidden behind a
thick veil of clouds. In 1993, *Magellan*
used radar to map the surface of Venus.
Astronomers discovered a strange
landscape of volcanoes, pancake-like
rock domes and lava flows.

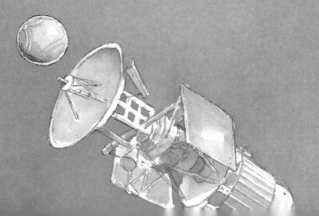

Mercury was visited by
Mariner 10 in 1974 and 1975.
Astronomers discovered that
the closest planet to the Sun
is covered with large craters
and deep cracks.

31

Discovering the universe

Next time you're walking on a sandy beach, think of this: the universe holds more stars than there are grains of sand on all the world's beaches. The vastness of space is hard to grasp, but powerful telescopes and computers help scientists understand the universe.

Space shuttle astronauts repair the Hubble Space Telescope in 1993.

Rescuing a dream

The Hubble Space Telescope was every astronomer's dream. Finally, with a telescope positioned above Earth's hazy atmosphere, people could see clearly into space. But soon after its 1990 launch into orbit around Earth, Hubble began to have problems. Instead of sending back clear pictures, the world's most expensive telescope was returning fuzzy photos. The dream was turning into a nightmare!

Fortunately, scientists tracked down the problem. One of the telescope's large mirrors could not focus light. Hubble was like a person who needs glasses to see properly.

NASA trained a crew of six men and one woman. On December 2, 1993, the astronauts soared into orbit in the space shuttle *Endeavour*. They caught up with Hubble, grabbed it with the shuttle's 16-m (52-ft.) robot arm and locked the telescope into the *Endeavour's* cargo bay.

In a series of space walks, the crew added ten small mirrors to correct the telescope's vision. They also replaced Hubble's solar panels, fixed its electronic system, installed a new camera and upgraded its computer.

The hard work paid off. Since the repair mission, Hubble has returned amazing pictures of our solar system, the Milky Way and other galaxies in the farthest regions of deep space.

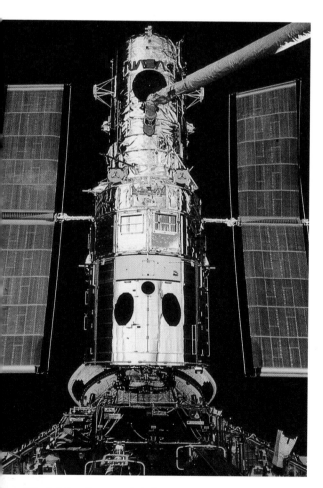

The Hubble Space Telescope is held in the space shuttle's cargo bay.

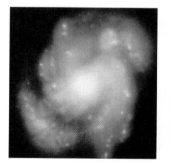 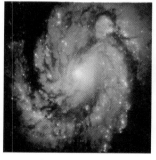

Here's how Hubble saw this galaxy before and after the repair mission.

How do modern astronomers learn about the stars?

Astronomers use powerful telescopes connected to computers and cameras. Some telescopes are on the ground. Others are in space.

Astronomers study a star's visible light (the glow we can see) and its invisible energy (including x-rays and radio waves). They learn what the star is made of, how far away it is and how fast it is traveling.

The Very Large Array is a huge collection of radio telescopes in New Mexico.

Observatories are often built on mountaintops. There, high above fog and pollution, astronomers can see the stars more clearly.

What have we learned about the universe?

We now know that the universe contains trillions of stars. Nearly all of them are found in large groups called galaxies that clump together in collections called clusters. Clusters of galaxies form even bigger collections called superclusters.

By studying the light of distant stars, astronomers know that the universe was once incredibly hot and dense. All matter and energy was squeezed into a space smaller than a grain of sand. About 10 to 15 billion years ago, it suddenly began to expand and cool in a process called the Big Bang. The universe is still expanding.

TRY IT!

Blow a bubble map of the universe

Clustered galaxies form patterns that astronomers compare to the sudsy structure of soap bubbles. You can create a similar image.

> **You'll need:**
> ○ an empty yogurt container
> ○ 125 mL (¼ c.) liquid dishwashing soap
> ○ 15 mL (1 tbsp.) powder paint
> ○ a spoon
> ○ a straw
> ○ a large sheet of paper

1. Pour the dishwashing soap into the yogurt container. Add the powder paint. Mix well.

2. Blow through the straw into the soap mixture. Keep blowing until the bubbles rise above the top of the container.

3. Lightly lower the paper onto the bubbles. Do not press down.

4. Remove the paper and look at the pattern. Imagine that each line holds thousands of galaxies. That's billions of stars!

This map shows the pattern formed by 1065 galaxies in one small slice of the universe.

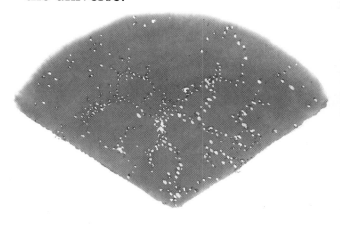

Will people ever travel to the stars?

After the Sun, the nearest star to Earth is Proxima Centauri. It is 40 trillion km (25 trillion mi.) away. In a modern spacecraft, the journey to Proxima Centauri would take more than 50 000 years.

Other stars are hundreds and thousands of times farther away. Even if you could somehow travel at the speed of light, a trip to one of them would take many lifetimes.

Right now, star travel happens only in science-fiction books and movies. Still, future technology might make this fantasy come true.

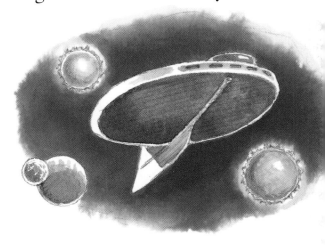

SPACE DATA

In 1900, the largest telescope in the world was the 1-m (40-in.) telescope at Yerkes Observatory in Wisconsin. Today, the world's largest telescope is the 10-m (400-in.) Keck Telescope on Mauna Kea in Hawaii.

In 1999, astronomers discovered three giant planets orbiting the distant star Upsilon Andromedae.

By studying the light from different galaxies, Edwin Hubble discovered in 1929 that all galaxies are moving away from one another in every direction. (In other words, the universe is expanding.) The Hubble Space Telescope is named after this famous astronomer.

Space exploration timeline

Here are some major steps we've taken in our quest to learn about space.

1610
Galileo Galilei uses one of the first telescopes to discover Jupiter's four largest moons.

1781
William Herschel discovers Uranus.

1846
Astronomers in Berlin discover Neptune.

1929
Edwin Hubble presents evidence that the universe is expanding.

1930
Clyde Tombaugh discovers Pluto.

1957
The Soviet Union launches the first artificial satellite, *Sputnik 1*.

1961
Soviet cosmonaut Yuri Gagarin is the first person to fly in space.

1963
Soviet cosmonaut Valentina Tereshkova is the first woman in space.

1969
American astronaut Neil Armstrong is the first person to walk on the Moon.

1974
Mariner 10 visits Venus and Mercury.

1976
Vikings 1 and *2* land on Mars.

1979
Pioneer 11 flies by Saturn.

1981
Columbia completes the first space shuttle mission.

1986–89
Voyager 2 passes Uranus and Neptune.

1990
The Hubble Space Telescope is launched into orbit around Earth.

1990
Ulysses is launched on a mission to study the Sun.

1992
Construction of the 10-m (400-in.) Keck Telescope begins.

1994
The *Galileo* probe takes pictures as a comet smashes into Jupiter.

1996
The *Near-Earth Asteroid Rendezvous* (NEAR) spacecraft is launched.

1997
Cassini sets out to study Saturn and its moons.

1998
Astronauts begin assembling the International Space Station.

1999
The *Stardust* mission is launched to collect comet dust.

2004
The *Cassini* probe is scheduled to reach Saturn.

Will people ever live in space?

Astronauts have already lived on space stations for several months at a time. Scientists are now working on plans for a Moon colony, though it may not be built for a long time. People also dream of living on Mars. Some even suggest changing the Martian environment to make it more like that of Earth. While these ideas seem like science fiction now, some may come true in your lifetime.

What space mysteries remain?

Many questions about space are still unanswered. What is Pluto like? Does life exist on other planets? How many galaxies are there? Will the universe continue to expand forever? Some of these space mysteries may soon be solved. Others will never be explained. Like the people of long ago, we stare at the sky and wonder, "What's out there?"

Glossary

astronomer: someone who studies the stars, planets and other objects in space

Big Bang: the sudden expansion of the early universe from a tiny, hot lump of matter

comet: a ball of ice and dust that orbits the Sun

concave: curving inward. The inside of a bowl is concave.

constellation: a group of stars forming an imaginary picture

convex: curving outward. The outside of a bowl is convex.

digital: in short, separate pulses

galaxy: a vast collection of stars, gas and dust held together by gravity

gas: a form of matter made up of tiny particles that are not connected to one another and so can move freely in space. Air is made up of gases.

gravity: an invisible force that pulls objects toward one another

lunar: of the Moon

Milky Way: the galaxy in which we live; also, the hazy band of light our galaxy forms in the night sky

nucleus: the central core of a comet or other object

planet: a large object that orbits a star and does not make its own light

radio waves: an invisible form of energy, often emitted by stars

reflect: to bounce light waves back in the direction they came from

refract: to bend light waves

rocket: a machine propelled by escaping gases

satellite: an object that orbits a larger object in space. The Moon is Earth's natural satellite. A space station is an artificial satellite.

space probe: a robotic spacecraft with no crew

space shuttle: a reusable spacecraft

space station: an orbiting space laboratory where astronauts work and live for weeks or months at a time

star: a glowing ball of superhot gases

universe: everything that exists, including billions of galaxies

weightlessness: when objects and people float freely in space

x-ray: a type of energy emitted by stars

Answers

Page 19: To find your weight on the Moon, divide your Earth weight by 6.

Page 27: You should see this:

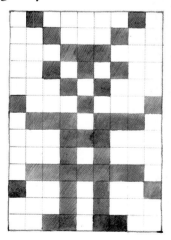

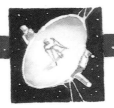

Index